# Who Is
# Greta Thunberg?

# Who Is Greta Thunberg?

by Jill Leonard

illustrated by Manuel Gutierrez

Penguin Workshop

PENGUIN WORKSHOP
An Imprint of Penguin Random House LLC, New York

Visit us online at www.penguinrandomhouse.com.

Library of Congress Cataloging-in-Publication Data is available upon request.

ISBN 9780593225677 (paperback)        10 9 8 7 6 5 4 3 2 1
ISBN 9780593225684 (library binding)   10 9 8 7 6 5 4 3 2 1

# Contents

# Who Is Greta Thunberg?

On August 20, 2018, a Monday morning in Stockholm, Sweden, a girl in a blue hoodie and yellow raincoat hopped on her bike and rode from her home to the Swedish parliament building—the meeting place of the country's government. She was barely five feet tall and wore her hair in two long braids.

Her name was Greta Thunberg. She was fifteen years old, and she was skipping school.

Was she doing it for fun?

No. Just the opposite. She had a very serious purpose. She was going to the government building to protest what she saw as a deadly climate crisis. A few months before, a newspaper had run an essay she wrote about her fears for the environment. "I want to feel safe," she wrote.

"How can I feel safe when I know we are in the greatest crisis in human history?" So, she decided to take action.

Greta brought a hundred flyers to give out to people. She also had a wooden sign that her father

had helped her make. It was painted white and in large black letters, the message in Swedish read: "School Strike for Climate." Her strike meant that, in protest, she refused to go to school.

This was the very first day of her strike.

Greta sat against a wall of the parliament building. She had tried to convince other young people she knew to join her. But nobody had. Greta was on her own.

All day long, people passed by her. If they noticed her sign, they didn't ask about it. Nobody took a flyer, either. The next day, however, there she was. Back at the same spot. For a while, a young man talked to her about her protest. He gave her a piece of chocolate, which Greta appreciated. But no crowd joined her.

Like so many teenagers born in the twenty-first century, Greta understood the power of social media. She posted a photo of herself holding her sign on Instagram and Twitter. She contacted a few Swedish newspapers to tell them about her strike to call attention to climate change. Sure enough, a couple of local papers sent reporters.

After that, Greta's strike started to grow.

More and more young people joined Greta at the parliament building. Like her, they wanted the Swedish government to take action by passing laws that would help reverse global warming. The planet needed saving. It was Greta's belief that grown-ups were the problem. They weren't doing what was necessary to save the planet. Young people needed to make them see that. Or else, what kind of future would they have?

# CHAPTER 1
## How It All Began

Greta Thunberg (say: TOON-berg) seemed to have everything a child could want in life. She had loving and creative parents. Her mother, Malena Ernman, was a well-known opera singer. Her father, Svante (say: SVAN-tay), was a writer and actor. Her little sister, Beata, was three years younger and looked up to Greta. And then there was Moses, Greta's adored golden retriever, and later on, a rescue dog named Roxy.

The family lived in a large house at the top of a hill in the beautiful city of Stockholm. Whenever the Thunbergs wanted peace and quiet, it was only a quick trip to their weekend home on an island named Ingaro.

Greta's parents had always taught Greta and Beata to be responsible about the environment. They turned off lights that didn't need to be on. They didn't waste water. They often rode bikes instead of taking their car. And when electric cars became available, they bought one.

Sensitive, smart, and serious, Greta liked horses, dogs, ballet, and learning to play the piano. For companionship, she often turned to books. And she was a deep thinker who sometimes seemed more like a grown-up than a kid.

# Sweden

Stockholm is the capital of Sweden, a country on the Scandinavian Peninsula in the very north of Europe. The winters are long and cold; the summers are short and mild. Sweden has more islands than any other country in the world—more than two hundred thousand! The city of Stockholm spreads across fourteen of them.

Sweden has a constitutional monarchy and a parliamentary system. That means there is either a king or queen with little power. The actual passing of laws is done by the elected members of the government, known as Parliament. The head of Parliament is called the prime minister.

Then, when she was eight, something happened in school that changed Greta's life.

Her class watched a film about global warming—how the earth's average temperature was rising to a point that it was causing terrible harm to the planet. It was the reason why extreme flooding and dangerous dry spells had become much more common, as well as violent hurricanes and uncontrollable fires.

From the film, Greta learned that ice caps at the North and South Poles were melting. This was dangerous for polar bears, which all live in countries near the Arctic Circle. To find food, polar bears must swim from one sheet of floating ice to the next. Because of ice melting, the distance between these sheets of ice was greater. It was harder for the polar bears to make it from one sheet to the next. Many weren't finding enough food to eat.

It upset everyone in the class to learn about

this. But after the film was over, the other children were able to go on with the rest of their days. Not Greta. All she could think about was the polar bears. If global warming was the problem, why was no one stopping it?

Greta's worrying grew worse and worse. By the time she was eleven, all she could think about was global warming. She stopped eating. She stopped playing the piano. She stopped going to school. She even stopped talking. For hours, she would just sit with Moses, petting and stroking his fur.

Malena and Svante tried everything to encourage Greta to eat more. They offered her favorite foods, such as avocados and little potato dumplings. But nothing worked. Greta lost more than twenty pounds. Svante described this time as "the ultimate nightmare for a parent." His child was suffering, and he wasn't able to help her!

# CHAPTER 2
## An Answer

After two months, Greta was no better. Her parents wanted to know what was wrong, so they took her to a children's hospital in Stockholm. A doctor there performed many tests, and fortunately, they *did* point to an answer, but a surprising one: Greta had Asperger's syndrome.

Asperger's syndrome is a mild form of autism. (It turned out that Greta's sister, Beata, also had Asperger's.) Many kids with Asperger's syndrome or autism are talented in certain areas, including math or music. But social situations can be difficult for them. They find it hard to make friends and have to learn things that other kids just seem to know—for instance, that it makes people uncomfortable if someone stands too close to them while talking.

With the doctor's help, Greta began to get better. She started to speak and eat again. She ate the same thing every day—pancakes filled with rice. And she wanted to eat by herself. Still, she was improving.

Learning that she had Asperger's syndrome made complete sense to Greta. It explained why she saw everything in life as being black or white— meaning, things were either right or wrong. In speeches, Greta has called having Asperger's her "superpower." It made her able to put so much focus and energy into a single problem—saving the planet.

An interest in the environment ran in Greta's family. A distant relative had been a famous scientist. His name was Svante Arrhenius. In the very late 1800s, he was among the first to explain what he called the greenhouse effect.

Svante Arrhenius

And he predicted that there would be global warming because factories and cars and trains were releasing so much carbon dioxide into the atmosphere.

Returning to school wasn't easy for Greta. Other kids were sometimes mean. They didn't understand why Greta spoke so softly and often didn't answer them. They thought she was being snobby. Greta, however, has often said, "I only speak when it is necessary." That is another symptom of her Asperger's syndrome.

Greta avoided other kids by spending recess and lunchtime in the school library. At times, her teacher came and helped her make up the work that she had missed. But that wasn't hard for Greta. Besides being smart, she has an extraordinary memory. It means that if she read something once, she remembered it in great detail.

Greta also read as many books on the environment as she could, including one written by her ancestor Svante Arrhenius. She learned much more about what started global warming. And she wondered: *Is there anything that can be done to reverse the damage done to the planet?*

# The Greenhouse Effect

Unlike other planets in our solar system, the earth is blanketed in a thick layer of invisible gases called the atmosphere. Some of the gases in the atmosphere, such as carbon dioxide, trap in heat from the sun. This is a good thing—as long as there isn't too much of it. Carbon dioxide keeps the earth warm enough—both day and night—for plants and animals, including humans, to live. The atmosphere works like the glass roof of a greenhouse that holds in heat allowing the plants inside to grow even during the coldest winter days.

# CHAPTER 3
## Changing Times

Greta had started learning about the environment when she was only about seven or eight. In time, she knew so much about this topic that, on a school trip to a museum exhibit about global warming, Greta even was able to spot some errors in the information about the display! She was so upset that she left the exhibit and waited outside for her teacher and the other students.

From all her reading, Greta understood global warming had started about two hundred years earlier, with the start of the industrial era in the mid-nineteenth century. Machinery that used fossil fuels—coal, oil, and some natural gases— was the root of the problem. The carbon dioxide the machines released stayed trapped in the atmosphere, which held in too much heat from the sun and made temperatures rise around the globe.

To Greta, that explained why, in Sweden, the summer of 2018 had been unusually warm. There had also been terrible forest fires in the north of her country that summer.

Greta also learned from books about the pre-industrial era, which lasted from about 1750 to 1850. During that era, most people were farmers. And when anyone traveled, it was on a horse. Practically everything that people used in their daily lives, including tools and clothes, was made by hand—either at home or in small workshops.

Then, Greta learned, by 1760, the Industrial Revolution began. The beginning of this era was marked by the invention of an improved steam engine. It meant items that were once produced by hand were being made in factories with the help of powerful machinery. They could produce things quickly and in large quantities. The machines, however, needed a fuel to power them, like coal. But burning coal released large amounts of carbon dioxide into the atmosphere. This would have terrible consequences for the planet.

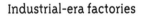

Industrial-era factories

By the end of the 1800s, horses were beginning to be replaced by cars. Instead of coal, car engines used gasoline or diesel fuel, which also spews carbon dioxide into the atmosphere.

Greta learned that the Industrial Revolution was when (most recently) the average global temperature started to rise because of all the carbon dioxide released by cars and factories. The earth has reached a point where the past ten years have been the hottest on record.

All her reading informed the way that Greta spoke about the warming, comparing it to a house.

"Our house is on fire," she has said many times.

So, were leaders of the world doing anything to put the fire out?

# CHAPTER 4
## What Is the World Doing?

Since the end of the 1970s, leaders of countries all around the world had been meeting to figure out how to prevent further damage to the planet. The answer was to reduce the amount of carbon dioxide released into the atmosphere. But the answer meant getting people to change their modern way of life. It meant getting many businesses to change how they made their products.

The most recent worldwide gathering took place in 2016 in Paris, France. Representatives from 197 nations—every nation in the world— came together. In time, all signed an agreement to address climate change.

The participants did not pass laws but

instead set goals for the countries of the world to reach. The main goal was to limit the global temperature from rising more than two degrees Celsius from pre-industrial temperatures. (Like Fahrenheit, Celsius is a form of recording temperature, but it uses a different scale. For instance, on the Celsius scale, 0 marks the freezing point, whereas 32 is the freezing point in Fahrenheit.) The participants agreed this goal should happen by 2050 at the latest, noting that 2030 would be a much safer deadline.

To limit this global rise in temperature, many changes would need to take place. For instance, big corporations would have to manufacture less plastic and rely less on fuels like oil and coal to lower their carbon dioxide production.

In her speeches and in her writing, Greta tried to explain why even small rises in global temperature—like two degrees Celsius (3.6 degrees Fahrenheit)—had big consequences. They could make sea levels rise, which would cause changes to both the climate and the geography of the planet. Changes that might never be undone.

So, has the Paris Agreement produced any results?

Yes.

China, for example, decided to scrap plans for more than one hundred coal-fired power plants. It is investing in new energy sources and has a strict national plan for reducing the release of carbon dioxide. This is important because China is the second biggest user of fossil fuel energy in the world. (The United States is the first.)

Greta knew about the goals of the Paris Agreement, but to her, having goals wasn't as good as enacting laws. And that wasn't happening fast enough. She didn't think her own country's government was doing nearly enough. If adults weren't taking action on their own, then maybe it was up to young people to make them— young people like Greta herself.

# CHAPTER 5
## On Strike

Meanwhile, in the United States, on February 14, 2018, at Marjory Stoneman Douglas High School in Florida, a former student entered the school with a powerful gun and opened fire on students and staff members. Seventeen people were killed.

When Greta learned that teenagers in Florida were protesting gun violence, she took notice.

There had been many mass shootings before in the United States, and yet the government had not passed a single new law to make it illegal to own the most dangerous types of firearms. The students at Marjory Stoneman Douglas decided to skip school and go on strike. It was their way of saying to the US government: "Do something!"

Greta decided to follow their example. That August, she began her own strike against the Swedish government's inaction on climate change. Every day for three weeks, she stood outside Stockholm's parliament building, wearing a yellow raincoat and holding a sign that read "School Strike for Climate" in Swedish.

On September 9, 2018, there would be elections for members of Parliament. She took photos of the strike each day and kept a diary about what she was doing on Instagram. By election day, about a hundred people had joined Greta. Like her, they hoped the protest would make climate change an issue.

It didn't, unfortunately. But Greta's strike did not end.

At first, Greta's parents had not been in favor

of her strike. Like her teachers, they thought getting an education was more important. But Malena and Svante came to see how the strike was making Greta a much stronger person. They also listened to all the facts about climate change that she knew.

Greta's passion made them change their own behavior. They gave up flying on airplanes because planes use an enormous amount of diesel fuel. That was hard for Malena because it meant she couldn't perform in operas in faraway cities. Like Greta, Svante stopped eating meat. That was because meat has to be sent by truck from farms or meat-packing plants to supermarkets. Like planes, trucks emit high amounts of carbon dioxide. And instead of buying vegetables from a supermarket, Greta and her family planted their own garden.

After the disappointing Swedish elections,

Greta decided to change the way her strike worked. From then on, she would strike only on Fridays. Fridays for Future, she named the movement. The other weekdays she would spend in school.

Perhaps, this was the beginning of the end of her strike.

# CHAPTER 6
## A Movement Is Born

But her new plan was not the beginning of the end! A movement was growing. Strikes began in other cities and towns in Sweden. Then in other countries in Europe. In Belgium, thirty-five thousand schoolchildren went on strike, refusing to go to school. When a government official mocked them, the public outcry was so great against her that she had to resign.

Requests began coming in for Greta to give speeches to other protest groups. In October, the Thunbergs drove in their electric car for more than twenty hours to reach London, England.

In front of the British Parliament, Greta told the adults in the crowd: "When you think about the future, you don't think beyond the year 2050.

By then, I will, in the best case, not even have lived half my life. What happens next? In the year 2078 I will celebrate my seventy-fifth birthday. What we do or don't do will affect

my entire life, and the lives of my children and grandchildren. We already have all the facts and solutions. All we have to do is wake up and change."

Greta was invited to attend an important meeting to be held in January 2019 in Davos, Switzerland, an Alpine resort town. Ordinary citizens cannot just show up at the Davos meeting. Receiving an invitation is a big deal. Every year, the most powerful government leaders and world figures meet there for several days to talk about problems threatening the global economy.

To get to Davos, Greta and Svante traveled for thirty-two hours on a train. (A plane would have gotten them there in just a couple of hours, but Greta wouldn't fly.) And instead of checking into a fancy hotel, Greta and her father stayed in a tent, enduring freezing temperatures. Talk about not wasting energy!

It was her speech at Davos that turned Greta Thunberg into a superstar. A girl who did not like to speak unless it was absolutely necessary gave a four-minute speech. Her sincerity, passion, and honesty captured the audience. She said that even though there was snow and ice on the ground, the world was on fire. And action was needed. When she finished, everyone including Bono, the famous lead singer of the Irish rock band U2, stood and applauded.

Davos was just the beginning.

Greta Thunberg was thrust onto the world stage.

On September 23, 2019, she spoke before the United Nations (UN) in New York City.

The UN is an organization of almost all the nations in the world. It tries to help countries work together to prevent wars from breaking out. It also helps wherever there is an emergency—a bad outbreak of a disease or a natural disaster like an earthquake.

Greta and Svante arrived in New York City in late August, after two weeks aboard a sleek gray sixty-foot racing boat. It was called the *Malizia II*, and it saved energy in every way possible. Its electricity came from solar panels. It traveled under sail. There weren't even toilets—only buckets at the back of the boat!

A crowd was waiting in New York Harbor to greet Greta. It had been about a year since she first stood with her white sign outside the parliament building in Stockholm. Since then, she had become the voice of a movement, a *big* movement. In New York, earlier that year, an estimated 250,000 people had marched to City Hall to protest climate change; 100,000 had gathered in London by the famous clock tower called Big Ben; and almost half a million people raised their voices in more than six hundred German cities and towns.

For her speech at the United Nations, Greta appeared in the same kind of outfit she always wore—sneakers, pants, a plain long-sleeved top. If the audience expected a calm list of environmental dangers, they were in for a surprise.

At times, Greta seemed barely able to hold back tears.

Asked what was her message to world leaders, Greta replied: "We'll be watching you." She meant that young people would be watching to see whether real action on climate change happened. Then she told the audience, "This is all wrong. I shouldn't be up here. I should be back in school . . ." Several times, Greta said,

"How dare you?" She couldn't understand how grown-ups could sit around, worrying about making more money while "entire ecosystems are collapsing."

Greta's speech made headlines in newspapers around the globe.

But did everyone consider her a hero?

No. Nor did everyone fear for the planet's future. Donald J. Trump, the president of the United States, has called climate change a "hoax"—a joke. Even though it is not, in 2017, President Trump announced that the United States was pulling out of the Paris Agreement.

There are some scientists who point out that over its long history, Earth has weathered through other "hot" periods. An overwhelming number of climate experts, however, think that this most recent global warming is different and more dangerous because it is human made.

As for Greta, she has no doubts about the danger we face. And she has brought attention to the environment in a way that no one before has been able to do. In December 2019, *Time* magazine featured her on the cover and named her Person of the Year.

In recent years, other people who have received this recognition include former US president Barack Obama, Chancellor Angela Merkel of Germany, and Pope Francis. Early in 2020, Greta was nominated for the Nobel Peace Prize, an honor that is awarded to someone who has fought to make the world a better place, for the second time.

It remains to be seen what the world will do to meet the goals set by the Paris Agreement. Greta doesn't think well-meaning individuals, just by themselves, can stop the problem. She believes that governments have to work together to create solutions. And they must act quickly. Still, as she has said herself, "You are never too small to make a difference."

# Timeline of Greta Thunberg's Life

| | |
|---|---|
| **2003** | Born in Stockholm, Sweden |
| **2005** | Sister, Beata, is born |
| **2018** | Begins her school strike on August 20 |
| | Elections are held for Swedish Parliament on September 9, but those elected didn't regard climate change a priority |
| | Returns to school in September, striking only on Fridays |
| **2019** | Speaks at the World Economic Forum held in Davos, Switzerland, in January |
| | Nominated for the Nobel Peace Prize |
| | Arrives in New York City aboard the *Malizia II* on August 28 |
| | Speaks before the United Nations in New York City in September |
| | Named *Time*'s Person of the Year in December |
| **2020** | Nominated for the second time for the Nobel Peace Prize |